Practical Jokes

Practical Jokes

A comic guide to wonderfully wicked tricks and gimmicks that are guaranteed to cause a riot of fun

JON TREMAINE

p

About the Author

Jon Tremaine has 28 non-fiction books to his credit covering subjects as many and varied as magic, astrology, origami and backgammon. He has been a professional magician for over 30 years, and lives in Sussex with his wife Suzy.

This is a Parragon Publishing Book
This edition published in 2004

Parragon Publishing
Queen Street House, 4 Queen Street
Bath BA1 1HE, UK

Copyright © Parragon 2000

Designed, packaged and produced by
Stonecastle Graphics Limited
Cover design by Design Principals

All rights reserved. No part of this publication may be reproduced, stored in a retrieval system, or transmitted in any way or by any means, electronic, mechanical, photocopying, recording or otherwise, without the prior permission of the copyright holder.

ISBN 1-40540-319-5

All of the practical jokes in this book are intended to be safe and fun. The publishers and their agents cannot accept liability for any loss or damage caused by anybody attempting to recreate these suggestions.

Manufactured in China

Contents

Introduction

I have wanted to write this book for years –
ever since the days when I worked behind
the counter in a joke shop in London selling
stink bombs, itching powder, joke spiders,
and the like! Over these years I have been
the perpetrator and also the victim of many,
many practical jokes. It is with great
pleasure that I pass some of them on
to you now.

What is a Practical Joke?
Very simply, it is a trick of a humorous
nature that you play on a friend or
acquaintance. This book is not concerned
with cruel and dangerous practical jokes. To
be successful a practical joke has also to be
thought funny by the victim of the prank.

Sense of humor differs from person to person so you must be very careful in your choice of jokes. If you inadvertently offend someone, you must apologize immediately. It will not do to accuse the victim of lacking a sense of humor. You are in the wrong because you have chosen the wrong gag at the wrong time and perpetrated it on the wrong person.

Jokes that cause confusion rather than embarrassment are always best and I have chosen the gags in this book very carefully with this in mind. Some can be considered as "old classics" – like the Whoopee Cushion and the other wonderful gimmicks that come with this book. Others are quite new. All of them are guaranteed to cause a riot of fun!!!

Whoopee Cushion

Let's be totally honest with each other. Breaking wind is *funny* although at times it is also very smelly. Everybody does it – you do – so do your parents, your schoolteacher, the local policeman, your dog – even the Queen of England does it! The Whoopee Cushion breaks wind to order!

How It Works

When the inflated Whoopee Cushion is squeezed or depressed it makes a loud rasping noise as air is expelled through the flexible "neck" of the cushion.

The Booby-Trap

Blow a little air into the mouth of the Whoopee Cushion (not too much). Hide it under the normal cushion of a chair or sofa. When someone sits in the chair the cushion deflates with a very rude wind-breaking noise! It is funniest when everyone in the room knows that it is about to happen – everyone, that is, except the victim who chooses to sit in the booby-trapped chair.

You can pull the joke even if there aren't any cushions under which to hide the Whoopee Cushion. Just slip it under your arm inside your pullover or jacket. Get the "target" to sit between you and a friend who is also "in the know." Wait for a suitable quiet moment and then activate the cushion. Don't say anything. You and your friend should just turn to look at the "target" with disgusted looks on your faces.

Wind And Water

The cushion also works under water so you can have great fun when your parents are trying to hurry you out of the bathroom. Just let rip! The noise and water turbulence should send them scurrying out of the bathroom in a hurry!

Q: What do you call a mathematician who breaks wind in the bath and counts the bubbles?
A: A Puff Adder!

Black Face Soap

This is a piece of good-natured fun and excitement. Just leave the bar of black face soap in the bathroom and wait for the action.

The more a person washes with this special soap, the blacker they get!
You'll have great fun as you watch victims catch sight of their dirty faces in the mirror and wonder what on earth is happening. The joke soap contains harmless dye that can be easily washed off with ordinary soap and water.

Double-Sided Sucker

This little gimmick is one of the most versatile items in a practical joker's armory. Its uses are only restricted by the limits of your imagination.

Simply stated the double-sided sucker sticks nearly anything to nearly anything! Extra adhesion can be obtained by wetting the sucker surfaces before applying them to the objects.

Be careful not to use the sucker on an item that contains *hot liquid*. This could easily get spilt and scald the victim. Not nice!

One last little warning. Don't stick the sucker to your (or anyone else's) forehead or skin. They can be very difficult to remove and the sucker can bruise the skin.

Here are a few ideas for you to experiment with. Stick – a cup to a saucer – a glass to the bar – a spoon to a saucer – the soap to the bath – a book to a desk – books to each other – a coin to the sidewalk – the TV remote control unit to the table – a telephone to its cradle – a shoe to a wooden floor.

Vibrating Handshake

Wind up the vibrating handshaker. Slip the ring over your finger and conceal the "body" of the gimmick in your palm. Now when you shake hands with someone, the button will be depressed and a loud, whirring sound will be heard. The victim will feel a vibrating sensation and will imagine that he has received an electric shock.

That is the "classic" application of the gimmick. However, it can be used in many other ways:

Wind the gimmick up and activate the button yourself when...
...you do up your zip!
...as someone bends over!
...when you switch the light on or turn on any form of switch.
...you look behind the curtains – it will sound like a wasp!
...as you reach into a bag of candy – or a cookie jar – or a drawer – or your pocket – or inside your shirt to scratch.
...as the world's smallest CD player. Hold it to your friend's ear and press!

Have fun!

Water Pistol Fun

A great water pistol gag is to stand behind someone and pretend to sneeze. At the same time squirt a little water onto the back of their neck and quickly pocket the pistol before they turn around! They will think your sneeze has showered them.

You could also pretend that your pistol is bunged up and ask your friend if he can see anything stuck in the nozzle. Give him a good soaking as soon as he looks up the barrel!

Get a friend to balance an apple on his head. Tell him that you are going to emulate William Tell's famous feat of marksmanship by shooting the apple off the top of his head with your sharp-shooting pistol. Take aim and squirt him in the face!

Note: always use fresh clean water.

Clutching at Straws

Here are a couple of great practical jokes that involve the common-or-garden drinking straw:

Suck It and See

Try this when you are next in your local hamburger place with friends. When one of your pals goes to the toilet, take the lid off his drink, remove the straw, *tie a knot in it*, reinsert it through the hole in the lid and then snap the lid firmly in place again. Everything looks normal.

When your friend returns to the table, watch him struggle as he tries to finish his drink. It is hysterical!

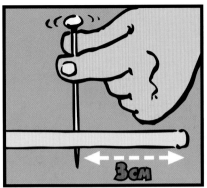 

A Real Sucker

If you get the chance to "doctor" everyone's drinking straws before a party – the resulting chaos can be very funny.

Make a pinhole about 1 inch (3cm) from each end of all the straws; push the pin right through so that holes are made on both sides. You must pierce both ends of the straws because you don't know which way round your friends will put them in their drinks. If the straws are individually wrapped, you can still do this by piercing through the wrapping paper too!

Enjoy the fun as everyone struggles to drink! You will be the only one who will be able to drink normally because you slyly cover the holes with your finger and thumb!

Piff-Paff-Puff

This is a great laugh! Take a deck of playing cards and turn the fourth card from the bottom *face up*. It will be the only card in the deck that is the wrong way round.

Stand facing your friend. Hold the deck in your right hand as shown. Say: "I want to show you a fantastic card trick that I have just learned and there is no way that *you* will be able to do it. You're just not smart enough!"

" Hold the deck up in front of his face showing the bottom card.
Say: "Piff"

" Hold the deck facing the floor.
Say: "Paff"

" Turn your wrist so that the bottom card faces you. Remember the name of the card. We will assume that it was the Four of Hearts.
Say: "Puff"

Hold the deck facing the floor again.
Say: "The Four of Hearts!"

Remove this card from the bottom and lay it aside after showing it.

Go through the "Piff–Paff–Puff" routine twice more, naming the correct cards and emphasizing all the time that your friend will not be able to do it because it is too difficult.

By the end of your third demonstration he will be just dying to have a go at this ridiculously stupid card trick.

He says, "Piff, Paff, Puff." However, when he gets to the "Puff" part of the trick he will be faced with the back of a playing card and not the face! He won't be able to name it!

His face will be "blank" too!

A Real Plateful

You will need to borrow two dinner plates for this great, but very naughty, practical joke.

All plates have slightly recessed bottoms. You will need to coat the recessed underside of one plate (but not the lip that sits on the table) with a thin layer of *jam*! When this is done, place both plates on the table and your secret preparation is complete.

When your friend arrives stand facing him. Tell him that you are going to carry out an observation test and he must copy your actions exactly.

Pick up both plates and hand him the unprepared one. You hold the other one in your left hand by its edge. Keep its jammy bottom hidden. Have him hold his plate in the same way. From now on he must do exactly as you do.

▶ Pass the plate from your left hand to your right hand.
▶ Pass it back into your left hand.
▶ Take it in your right hand again.

18

► Take it back in your left hand.

► Rest your right index finger on top of the plate and trace it around the center in a clockwise circle.

► Apparently push your finger up under the plate and inscribe a circle on its bottom. Just pretend to do this otherwise your finger will get covered with jam and spoil the gag. He follows suit with his plate – actually touching the bottom surface.

► Now rub your finger across your forehead from left to right.

► Make another circle under the plate again.

► Drag your finger down the left side of your face.

► Make another circle under the plate.

► Drag your finger down the right side of your face.

► Make yet another circle under the plate.

► Drag your finger down the bridge of your nose.

He duplicates all these actions. *Now swap plates!*

He now has the plate with the jammy bottom. Repeat the whole routine. Your friend will end up looking like a Native American complete with jammy war paint!

Don't tell him. Let him discover it for himself. Get your running shoes on!

You've Got It Taped

Here are two great gags using a small tape recorder. Both the jokes require you to pre-record a message on a blank tape – so make sure that it is truly blank and not someone's rare and precious recording!

Here, There, and Everywhere

Prepare for this stunt in your bedroom. Switch the tape to "Record" and stay quiet for about ten minutes. Stop the machine. Now set the machine to "Record" again and in an angry, startled voice record the following message:

"Come and look at this everybody. Who's been messing about in my room?
What a dump! Who's been drawing all over the walls?"

Now rewind the tape to the beginning. Set the volume to maximum and then press "Play."

Immediately go downstairs with a book and sit quietly in a corner – reading and minding your own business. Ten minutes later your message will boom through the house. The resulting chaos will be very, very funny.

Help!

Do you get dragged around the supermarket when your mother does the weekly shopping? Awful isn't it! Here's a great way to liven things up.

Make another time-delayed message. A couple of minutes should do nicely. Then record the following message in a panic-stricken terrified voice:

"Help! Help! Someone please help me. I'm trapped inside this shopping cart! Help!"

Switch the tape recorder on with the volume turned to maximum and secretly slip it into the shopping cart amongst all the shopping bags and boxes while your mother is deeply engrossed looking at her shopping list and the shelves of food.

You have two minutes to make yourself scarce!

Tearing Off a Strip

The best practical jokes are always very simple. This one came as a result of my interest in Origami – the ancient Japanese art of paper folding.

Take a sheet of white or cream plain paper – any size will do.

Fold it in half.

Tear out a pointed segment about 3in long.

Open it up and accordion-pleat the left-hand half, i.e. make a small fold at the end of the strip, turn it over and fold back the same amount of paper, turn the paper over again and fold the same amount again, continuing in this way until you reach the middle. Open up the folds a little and let it "hang loose."

Lick the underside of the unfolded half to moisten it – then press it onto a nice bold piece of wallpaper in a smart restaurant or the living room of a friend's house!

The illusion of ripped wallpaper is complete!

It also looks great stuck onto expensive leather-bound books and smart briefcases! Have fun.

Pharaoh's Finger

This will really make your friends jump! You will find the little bit of preparation required to carry out the joke well worthwhile.

Take an old matchbox and cut a slot in the cover and a hole in the drawer as shown - then assemble the two sections.

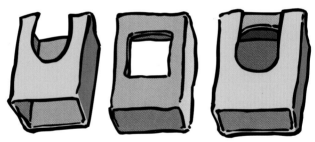

Now hold the box as shown and stick your index finger through the hole and into the box, curling it so that it points back toward your body. Slowly open the box and you can show a finger lying inside! Pack some shredded paper or tissue around the finger and dab a few drops of red ink around the edges to simulate blood.

Finish it off by decorating the outside of the box with Egyptian-style hieroglyphics.

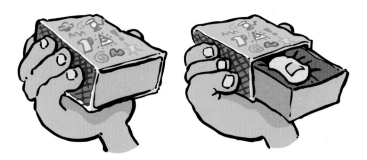

Tell your friend that you dug up this little box in your garden and you think that it must be a relic left over from an Ancient Egyptian pharaoh's tomb. Open the box to show the phantom finger. Ask him to stroke it five times for luck. Wiggle your finger violently on the fifth stroke and your friend will jump through the ceiling!

Movie Moths

Try this if you get the chance! Using a butterfly net I once collected about 30 moths over the course of a weekend. I kept them in a shoe box with holes punched in it so they had plenty of air to breathe and were well-ventilated.

On Halloween night I suddenly had the bright idea of taking the creatures to see a movie at our local film theater. Once the movie was well underway, I lifted the lid of the shoe box and let all the moths out.

You can imagine the chaos it caused because the moths – attracted by the light of the projector – all flew toward it and they proceeded to cast huge, eerie, bat-like shadows across the screen as they flitted in front of the lens. Creepy!

Q: Why did the monkey fall out of the tree?
A: Because it was dead!
Q: Why did the second monkey fall out of the tree?
A: Because he was holding hands with the first monkey!
Q: Why did the third monkey fall out of the tree?
A: Because he thought it was a game!

X-Ray Sunglasses

The funniest card stunt ever! Everyone is "in" on the joke – except the poor victim who is convinced that he can read the identity of each playing card from the back when he wears your "special" sunglasses.

You need:
An old deck of cards
A pair of sunglasses
A black felt marker pen

Take the 2♥; 4♠; 6♦; and any other card and put them to one side.
Boldly mark the rest of the cards on their backs like this:

The Ace of Hearts = AH; the King of Clubs = KC; the Nine of Diamonds would be 9D; the Jack of Spades would be JS; etc.

Assemble the deck again and put the remaining four unmarked cards on top. From the top they are the 2♥; 4♠; 6♦ and the other card. *You must memorize the names of the first three cards!* This should be very easy for you.

Sit talking to your friend. You say that you have got this fantastic deck of "marked cards." You can tell what they are from the backs! The only snag is that you have to look at them through a special pair of X-ray sunglasses.

Put the sunglasses on and pick up the deck of cards. Peer at the deck and say "The Two of Hearts." Turn the top card over and show that you are correct. Lay it to one side. Peer at the back of the next card – then say: "This is the Four of Spades!" Show that you are correct. The next card you say is "The Six of Diamonds! Isn't that amazing! Would you like to try?"

As he is putting on the sunglasses, take the next unmarked card off the top of the deck and put it on the bottom. Now a boldly marked card is on top but you must pretend that you cannot see the marking.

Tell your friend to look at the top card and try to name it. He does! and turns it over! You say "Correct!" Show the next card. He names it correctly. Stop after he has "read" about 12 cards.

You can now either let him in on the secret or switch the marked deck for an identical one without any markings! His amazing gift will apparently have deserted him and he will be none the wiser!

Sky High Flies

Joke plastic flies can be bought very cheaply in any novelty shop and they can be used in many marvellously malicious ways!

Drop one in your friend's bowl of soup.
Stick one in the pat of butter.
Put one inside your refrigerator (imagine your mother's face)!
Stick one on a mirror or a windowpane.
Fix one on your school shirt!
Stick one on your tongue (much better than a tongue stud)!

By far the funniest fly joke needs at least six flies. Use more if you can get them. The gag needs a room with a ceiling fan. There may even be one on your kitchen ceiling.

There will almost certainly be one in a room at school. Physicians' and dentists' waiting rooms nearly always have such a fan, as do many hotels.

With the fan switched off and in a stationary position, distribute the flies *on top of* the rotor blades. *Do not attempt to do this while the fan is buzzing around, you idiot!* We don't want chopped-up fingers, do we?

The next time someone switches on the overhead fan the flies will scatter everywhere – dive-bombing the unsuspecting people in the room!

Booby-Traps

Booby-traps can be funny – they can also be nasty! Do *not* balance a bucket of water on top of a partially opened door. This is a very dangerous stunt to pull because, apart from making someone terribly wet and causing a horrible mess, you could also give a person concussion if the bucket was to fall on his head! Not nice!

The Party Popper Bomb
(for doors that open outward)

You need:
*A party popper (of the type where you pull a detonator string; it then makes a loud bang and a shower of streamers is projected out of the plastic case into the air).
Sticky tape.
A length of string about 5–6 feet long.
A very heavy chair.*

Position the chair about threefeet from the door. Securely tape the party popper to one of the chair arms so that the popper is pointing directly at the door. Tie one end of the length of string to the detonator string, loop the string around the arm of the chair and then tie the other end to the doorknob!

When the door is pulled open by your unsuspecting victim, they will be met with a loud bang and a shower of streamers!

The Balloon Bomb
(for doors that open inward)

Simply blow up a balloon as full as it will go. Stick it securely to the door frame on the hinge side. (It's probably best to use a piece of removable adhesive compound to do this rather than sticky tape which can damage paintwork when it is pulled off.) That's it!

OK! How do you get out of the room after you've set the booby-trap? Through the other door of course! What if there isn't another door? Just stand outside the room as you are closing the door. Take up the slack in the string. Tighten and securely tie the string to the doorknob by reaching inside the small gap just before you close the door the last few inches!

Now when someone comes into the room, the balloon will be squashed in the inside edge of the door and explode with a deafening bang!

The Snowstorm

Here's how to create a surprise snowstorm and what happens if you swallow a swan!

Many of the best practical jokes are set up beforehand – like booby-traps. You may not always be around when the joke actually happens which, especially if the joke is particularly naughty, can be to your distinct advantage!

You need lots and lots of confetti or finely torn-up paper for this one. Simply tip the lot inside someone's folded umbrella! Next time they open up the umbrella they will get the surprise of their lives! The confetti will shower down upon them like a snowstorm. This gag works particularly well with the type of umbrella that springs open at the touch of a button.

I once tried this in a restaurant, secretly loading up a stranger's umbrella that he had left in the umbrella rack. The whole restaurant was in hysterics when the guy left, covering himself in "snow" on the pavement outside in the process.

Eating Swans

Writing about the snowstorm has reminded me of a great joke that you can play on a friend. Take two or three white paper tissues and shred them up into ragged pieces about 2in long. They don't have to be too exact. Squeeze them all together and hold them concealed in your right fist. You say:

"I've eaten some funny things in my time but last night's meal beats everything! We had **swan** for supper!"

"Really?"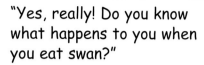

"Yes, really! Do you know what happens to you when you eat swan?"

"No."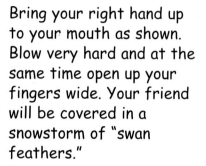

Bring your right hand up to your mouth as shown. Blow very hard and at the same time open up your fingers wide. Your friend will be covered in a snowstorm of "swan feathers."

Make that your swansong – and fly!

Bedtime Blues

Three lovely jokes to play on your brother or sister at bedtime. Great "get-your-own-back" stunts!

Perplexing Pajamas

Secretly sew up the ends of your brother's pajama trouser legs and pajama jacket sleeves. Just light tacking stitches will be sufficient to cause him no end of grief when bedtime comes around! And they are easy to get out without damaging the material of the pajamas when the joke is done.

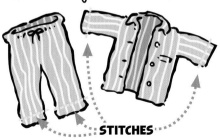

STITCHES

The Apple Pie Bed

This is one of the oldest known practical jokes, but it is still most effective!

Sometime during the day you take the opportunity to secretly remake the bed. Now when he tries to get into it – he can't! Half way is about the best he can manage!

The drawing makes it clear what you must do. The top

sheet is taken away and hidden. The bottom sheet is folded back up on itself. The blanket or duvet is then replaced and finally the end of the bottom sheet is folded over the blanket or duvet so that it looks like the folded-down end of the original top sheet. Wicked!

Inseparable

Your brother has gone to bed. His shoes are under it. Secretly tie the ends of the shoelaces to each other! And wait for the fun in the morning when he's struggling to get ready for school!

These jokes are individually very funny but when *all three are played together*, you will almost certainly have them begging for mercy!!!

Threadbare

This is my favorite practical joke. You *must* try it! All you need is a reel of white cotton.

Thread a needle with the end of the cotton and push it through the left lapel of your jacket from the inside to the outside. Pull a length of thread through and then remove the needle.

Wind the loose thread behind the lapel back on the reel and pop the reel into your outside breast pocket. The thread now runs secretly from your breast pocket – behind and through your lapel – leaving about 1 inch of cotton projecting from it and lying along the surface of the lapel. It should contrast with the jacket material so that it will show up nicely.

You must pretend not to notice it.

It won't be long before a well-meaning person will come along and try to remove the little cotton thread from your jacket lapel to keep you looking smart. Little? They find that they will have to pull more and more. The thread gets longer – and longer and LONGER!!! They end up with enough cotton to make a new shirt!

Even better: If you can borrow a little flat cotton bobbin from your mother's sewing machine, it will fit more easily into your breast pocket and so help conceal what's going on "behind the scenes."

Goldfish Gluttony

Eating your best friend's pet goldfish would not exactly make you the most popular person in the world! Fortunately it is just another fantastically funny practical joke!

This is what you do. Get a *carrot* and very carefully carve a rough goldfish-shaped slice from it. It need not be a work of art – just the general shape will do.

Hold your "carrot-fish" concealed in your hand. Look at your friend's aquarium or goldfish bowl and say:
"Wow! What beautiful fish! I just love goldfish. They are my favorite food!"

Pull your sleeve back and plunge your hand into the water. Stir it up a bit and then bring your hand out again displaying your imitation goldfish apparently held by its tail. Wiggle it about a bit and it will look just like a real one.

Throw your head back – open your mouth and drop the still wriggling goldfish into your mouth. Crunch it up with relish! Your friend will be going bananas!

Invisible Fish

A strategically placed goldfish bowl full of water but without any goldfish in it can be the source of great fun. When I worked in a joke shop we put one in the shop window with a sign that read **Invisible Fish**! It was meant purely as an eye-catcher. To our surprise a few people actually came in to purchase one. We sold them little bottles of water!

Let's Face It

Nosey Spoon

Balancing a teaspoon on your nose can become addictive! I have had whole restaurants full of strangers trying to do it before now. It looks quite ridiculous.

The spoon hangs from the end of your nose with the handle pointing downward. The secret is to warm the bowl of the teaspoon first by breathing on it. Tilt your head back and glide the bowl of the spoon slowly down the bridge of your nose.

Let go of the handle and the spoon should stay put. If at first you don't succeed – try, try, try again. It is a knack that you will quickly acquire.

Forehead Frolic

If you take a small coin and press it firmly to the center of your forehead, it will stick there. If you frown, it will fall off. Anyone can do this. It leads us into a lovely gag.

You need two identical small coins. Stick a drawing pin to one of them with double-sided sticky tape. Conceal the spiked coin in your left hand. Pick up the un-gimmicked coin and press it onto your forehead.

Challenge your friend to do the same. Frown, letting the coin drop into your cupped left hand, joining the spiked coin. Pick out the spiked coin with your right hand and pass it to your friend! Secretly pocket the other coin while your friend recoils in horror and inspects your forehead for pinholes!

Dumbo

Attach a strong cotton or nylon thread to the back of your ears with adhesive tape as shown in the illustration. Notice how the center part of the thread hangs down behind your back.

Ask your friend to waggle his ears! He can't, of course – but he may try, which can be hilarious! You then offer to demonstrate your own ear-waggling ability. Secretly put your hand behind your back and *gently* pull and release the thread a few times. Your ears will waggle about in a most peculiar way!

After doing this a few times, give the thread an extra hard pull. It will come clear from its fastenings and you can drop it on the floor, where it will remain unseen.

Book Bat

Book bats are wonderfully wicked creatures that you can plant in books all over the place! When the book is opened, the bat will fly out in a very scary way!

Photocopy or draw the bat shape illustrated on the last page of this book onto *thick* card. Cut out the shape and then cut the two slits on both wings. Fold the bat in half down the center. Get a small rubber band and slip it through the wing slots as shown.

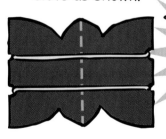

Open out the bat so that it is flat – thus stretching the rubber band quite taut. Place the bat inside a large book, ideally a hardback, near the center. The bat will fly into the air when the book is opened – scaring the pants off the reader!

Booby-Trap Birthday Cards

You can send a bat to a friend inside a birthday card. Alternatively you can rig the card with a metal washer and two rubber bands. Slit the card at top and bottom as shown. Loop the rubber bands onto the washer as illustrated and then slip the bands into the slots in the card.

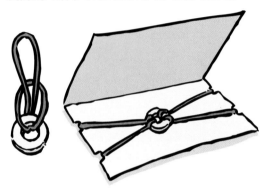

Now wind the washer round and round – at least 50 times – then close the card carefully and finally slip it into its envelope and mail it! The card will make a terrible rasping noise when your unsuspecting victim opens the birthday treat!

Coining It

If you act well enough and get the script right, this verbal trick can be a very funny scam.

Borrow two coins of the same value. Display them – one on each of your outstretched palms. Close your hands into fists. Turn your hands back-upward. Turn them over again. Open up your fists. Peer at each coin in turn. Gaze intently as if you were looking for a secret sign. Close your hands into fists and turn your hands back-upward again. Turn your hands over again and open up your fingers.

Peer at each coin intently again and then say "Which one of these two coins did you give me?"

The answer will be "I gave you both of them."

Say: "Thank you very much. That's very kind of you!" Drop the coins in your pocket and *run*!

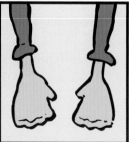

The Melting Spoon

If you can get your hands on an unwanted teaspoon, then this is a very "practical" practical joke!

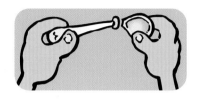

Hold the bowl of the spoon in one hand and the handle of the spoon in the other. Keep bending the spoon backward and forward until it snaps in two. It should break at its weakest point which is just below the bowl.

Now stick the two halves together again using a small piece of chewing gum. Do this as carefully as you can. You should be able to pick the spoon up without it falling apart, once the chewing gum has hardened.

When a friend comes to visit you, you offer him a nice cup of coffee. Ask him how many spoons of sugar he would like. Put the required number of spoonfuls in for him and *leave the spoon in the cup.* The hot liquid will soften the gum and, when your unsuspecting victim stirs up his coffee, he comes away with only the spoon handle. The bowl has apparently melted!

Dentist's Delight

Here are two ways to make your trips to the dentist more fun.

Open Wide

Cut an orange in quarters and eat the flesh of the orange. You are now going to make a cool set of false teeth from the skin left over. Take the skin of one of the quarters and cut a slit down the center. Then make five crosscuts to form the teeth as shown.

Turn the peel inside out so that the white side shows and slip the unit into your mouth – over your own teeth (if you have any!) and under both lips.

Now when the dentist says "Open wide," he will have the shock of his life!

Bridge That Gap

Next time you visit the dentist, try taking a small piece of black paper with you. Lick it and then press it onto your front tooth. It will stick to the tooth and make it look as if your front tooth is missing when you smile.

Q: I have two wristwatches. The battery in one of them has completely run down and the watch has stopped. The other watch gains one minute every hour. Which watch tells the correct time more often?

A: The watch that has stopped. It tells the correct time twice a day, while the other one is never right!

The Fakir's Forearm

Keep the secret of this practical joke to yourself. It's too good to share! You apparently stick a knitting needle straight through your forearm – wiggle the needle about showing that it really has gone right through – then pull the needle out again. You rub your arm vigorously and then let people inspect it. There are no marks – no wounds. Your skin has miraculously healed again!

How's it done?
A simple tube of any rubber adhesive solution is the answer! Coat a 2in square of the fleshy area inside your left forearm with rubber solution and allow it to dry. Once it is dry, it will be invisible.

Hold your arm with the treated side facing you. Pick up a large knitting needle and slide it vertically down the inside of your arm. From the spectators' point of view it must look as if you have pushed it through your arm. Once it appears to be firmly impaled half way through your arm, press the side of the needle onto the treated section of your skin and at the same time pinch the flesh

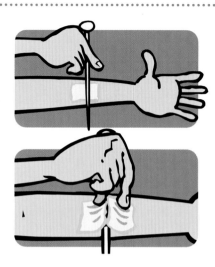

forearm back toward yourself and pull out the needle. If you now rub your forearm vigorously as if to take away the pain, the rubber solution will crumble into virtually invisible flakes and drop onto the floor unnoticed. You've destroyed the evidence of your trickery and no-one's any the wiser.

on either side of the needle and squeeze the two folds of flesh together over the needle. The rubber solution on each side will now grip and you can take your right hand away.

You can now show the front and back of your left arm to all the onlookers! It looks horrible! Wiggle the end of the needle a little for maximum effect! To finish, you turn your

It's a great illusion – the first time I did it a woman fainted!

This Little Piggy

This is naughty – but just the thing for that annoying younger brother or sister. You probably know the nursery rhyme that goes:

"This little piggy went to market,
This little piggy stayed at home,
This little piggy had roast beef,
This little piggy had none,
And this little piggy went
Wee-Wee-Wee all the way home."

You are supposed to touch a toe for each pig named. When you reach the last pig, you run your fingers up the child's body and tickle them under the arm. Yuk!

This is much more fun...!!! Photocopy the pig card illustrated five times onto white card and cut them out. Get a small piece of sponge and dip it in water so that it is wet, but not dripping. Hide the sponge in one of your hands.

Ask your victim to hold out his hand and start dealing the five pig cards onto his hand as you recite the rhyme:

"This little piggy went to market,
This little piggy stayed at home,
This little piggy had roast beef,
This little piggy had none,
And this little piggy went
Wee-Wee-Wee all the way home."

As you say the words, "Wee-Wee-Wee" *squeeze the sponge* onto his outstretched hand! Need I say more?!

Gotcha!

I.Q. Test One

Get your victim to stand on a stool and hold his hands out in front of him palm downward. Balance a glass of water on the back of each of his hands. The glasses should be full to the brim! The problem you confront him with is how to get out of the situation without spilling a drop. In all probability this will stump him and he will beg for you to help him escape.

In fact the answer is remarkably easy and if *you* find yourself in this situation, this is how you get out of it. Carefully raise your right hand until the glass is level with your lips. Drink the water and then grip the edge of glass between your teeth. This frees your right hand so that you can safely lift the glass that is on the back of your left hand. You're free!

I.Q. Test Two

If your victim is really obnoxious – try him with this!

You need a broomstick. Give it to him to hold. Fill a glass with water and, standing on a chair in order to reach high enough, press the mouth of the glass flat onto the ceiling. Now get him to raise the end of the broom handle upward and press it onto the bottom of the glass so trapping the glass against the ceiling.

Once he is set in this position, you jump down from the chair and leave the room, taking the chair with you! Even Einstein couldn't get out of that without having an accident!

How Long?

This practical joke is considered to be a classic. All you need is a ball of string and an unsuspecting passing acquaintance.

You stand outside a detached building that is bordered by roads on all four sides. Stand at one corner and wait for one of your friends' parents to come along. Approach the victim politely and say:

"I am sorry to bother you but could you help me please? I'm working on a school project and I have to measure this building. Please can you hold the end of this string for me?"

Give him the end of the string to hold and walk backward, away from him, until you are out of sight, playing out the string as you go. Circle around the building until you reach the far corner.

Tie the string to something strong and beat a hasty retreat to the next corner. From here you can carefully peek around the wall and gleefully watch what happens next!

Vanishing Corridor

This is a great way to use up your old newspapers! Cover a doorframe with newspaper by sticking the sheets together with sticky tape, and attaching the whole thing to the doorframe.

Now when someone opens the door, they will come face to face with a wall of newspaper!

Bet a friend that he can't fold a piece of newspaper in half ten times. He will fail because, strange as it may seem, it is impossible to fold a sheet of paper in half more than eight times. Try it!

A Lot of Dough

You break open your bread roll at dinner and to everyone's amazement you find a valuable coin inside it. Chaos follows as everyone tries to find money inside their own bread rolls. No such luck for them!

A little sleight of hand is called for. Don't panic! It couldn't be simpler. Conceal a large coin in your right hand. Pick up your bread roll with your left hand and place it in your right hand on top of the coin. The roll hides the coin from view.

Hold the roll with both hands as shown. Push the edge of the coin into the soft underside of the roll and at the same time break open the roll from the top in the normal way. You should now be able to see the edge of the coin in the roll.

Timing is essential to get the best effect. First say: "What on earth is this? I can't believe it! Look everybody!"

Now that you've got everyone's attention, you reach into your roll and pull out the coin.

"That's fantastic! I wonder if any of the other rolls have got coins in too?"

Don't get trampled in the rush!

Finger-Licking Good

This can be very funny if you present it in an off-hand way (excuse the pun). Snap off a piece of bread stick about as long as your finger. Jam it between your second and third fingers. It will look like a finger to a casual glance.

Suddenly say "Watch everybody!"

Hold your hand up in front of you as shown. Keep the 1st and 2nd fingers together and the 3rd and 4th fingers together. Pluck out the false finger and casually eat it!

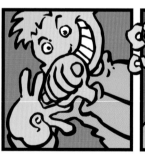

You will catch everyone off guard and, for a moment, they really will think that you have eaten your finger. Yuk!

Inflation

This is a great automobile joke. I would suggest that you do it on a neighbor's vehicle rather than your father's – thus avoiding a slap when the identity of the joker is discovered!

It's very simple. You need a good quality balloon and some sticky tape. Secretly stretch the balloon over the end of the muffler pipe and then bind the neck securely to the pipe with sticky tape.

That's it!

Now, when your neighbor starts his automobile, the exhaust fumes will fill the balloon and it will burst with a terrific bang!

Warning: Make sure that the vehicle has been standing stationary for some time and that the muffler is not hot before you attempt this gag!

The Old School Tie

Get hold of an old necktie that nobody wants. Undo the stitching and you will find that it has a plain white or off-white cloth lining inside. That's the part of the tie that you want.

When you are in the company of someone wearing a smart tie you can pull the following stunt. Concertina-fold the lining into a small bundle and conceal it in your right hand.

Stand in front of your victim and lift the end of his tie with your left-hand fingers as if you are admiring the pattern. Quickly bring your right hand up behind the tie so that it conceals your folded bundle and grip his tie with your fingers underneath and your thumb on top of it.

"What a beautiful tie! How long have you had it?"

"I got it for my birthday last month."

"I like the lining too!"

Reach underneath with your left hand and grip the end of your bundled-up lining. Pull down sharply. The lining will unfold and it will appear that you have ripped it clean out of the victim's tie!

Walk off saying, "Actually I like the lining better than the tie!!!"

Book Bat Template

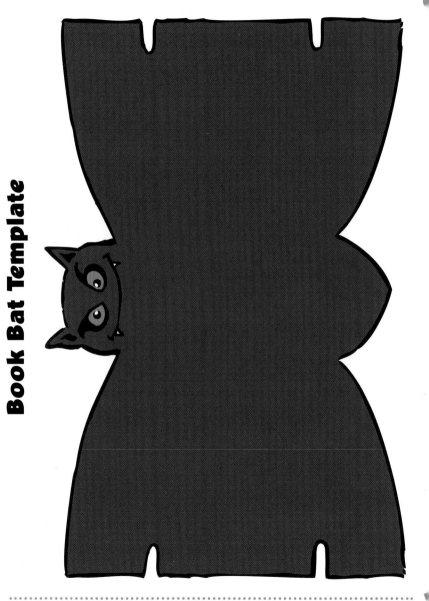